• THE PITKIN GU

A WART
CHRISTMAS
1939–1945

MIKE BROWN

The Second World War was a time of shortages, cutbacks and austerity – but for many people it was still important to celebrate Christmas, however difficult the circumstances. Of course, expectations during the 1930s and 40s were very different to today. Even before the war the philosophy of 'make do and mend' was a way of life for many families, and at Christmas gifts were fewer and festive fare simpler.

But in 1939, as the first Christmas of the war approached, there was much debate over how it should be celebrated. Little fighting had taken place and the German bombing offensive had not materialized, but the U-boat assault on Britain's merchant shipping had continued in earnest since the war started, and in November 1939 the government had announced that food rationing would begin in January. The blackout meant that brightly lit shop displays were banned, as were glimpses through house windows of Christmas trees and decorations.

All this, as well as the absence of those in the forces and of evacuated children, meant that Christmas would be somewhat muted. For some people this was not enough, their argument being that luxuries and conspicuous waste such as presents, cards, feasting, parties and dances should be sacrificed for the war effort. Even the old greeting 'Peace on earth, goodwill to all men' seemed inappropriate in wartime and began to be replaced by 'Peace to all men of goodwill'. Others reasoned that Christmas did not require conspicuous over-eating, drinking and spending, and that it was vitally important for the country's morale to remember what we were fighting for – and this view won.

As the war continued, however, and rationing, the Blitz and shortages tightened their grip, it would become increasingly difficult to celebrate Christmas. But in true wartime spirit, the British public refused to be downhearted and made the most of what little they had. This is the story of those six years of wartime Christmases, and how ways could always be found to celebrate this special time of year.

ABSENT FRIENDS

When war broke out in September 1939 the British army numbered around 865,000 men with 17,000 women in the auxiliary services. The National Service Act was passed on the first day of the war, and men aged 18 to 41 who were not in reserved occupations became eligible to be called up, although the first group of men aged 20 and 21 – the Militiamen – had been conscripted two months before war was declared.

Some 158,000 men of the British Expeditionary Force (BEF) were transported to France; by December most had taken up positions in the front line. On Saturday 9 December, Corporal Thomas W. Priday became the first British soldier to be killed in action in the Second World War.

▲ *This* Men Only *magazine from December 1942 shows a Royal Navy officer surrounded by presents. By that time, however, reality was very different; rationing, shortages and distance meant that gifts were few.*

However, September 1939 to April 1940 was the period of the 'Phoney War', when there was little military activity, and such incidents were uncommon.

On Christmas Day 1939 the men at the front were served traditional Christmas lunch, with one turkey for every 32 men, and one Christmas pudding for every 16. Newsreels of troops tucking in to their turkey dinners were filmed in advance so that families in Britain could enjoy their Christmas, feeling assured that 'the boys' were safe and well-cared for. The scene was repeated in military camps and hospitals throughout Britain.

Good advice

'Books are sure to be welcome, and pocket editions, rather than heavy and bulky volumes, and magazines and periodicals are in great demand. Pneumatic cushions which when not in actual use can be folded almost as flat as an envelope and can therefore be accommodated in a kitbag, cost very little, and may make an immeasurable difference to a man on active service.'

Good Housekeeping magazine, December 1939

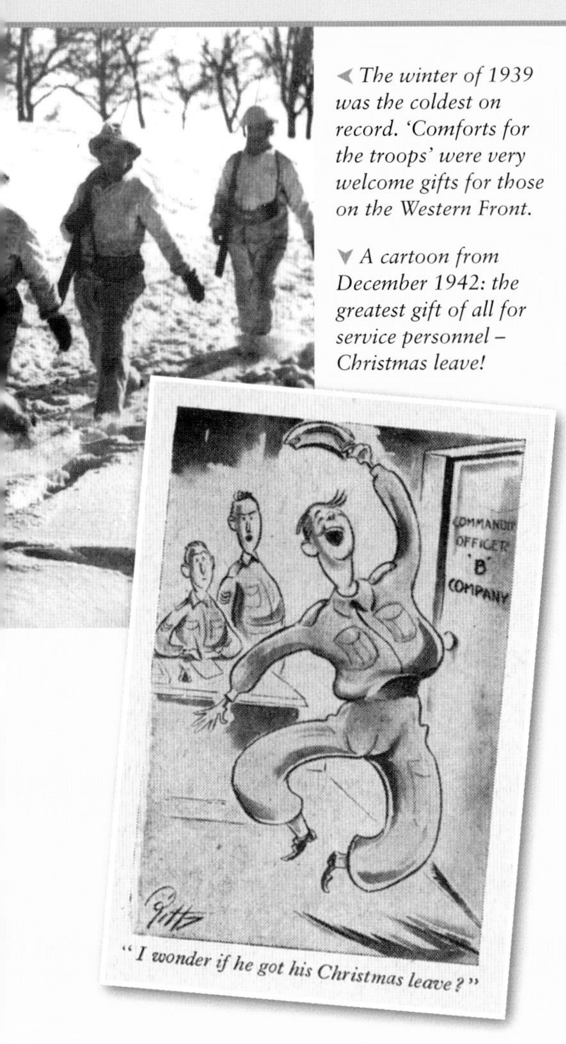

◀ The winter of 1939 was the coldest on record. 'Comforts for the troops' were very welcome gifts for those on the Western Front.

▼ A cartoon from December 1942: the greatest gift of all for service personnel – Christmas leave!

"I wonder if he got his Christmas leave?"

McConachies stew

The troops' turkey dinner of 1939 soon became a thing of the past. Gunner Michael Freeman of the 85th (Tees) Heavy Anti-Aircraft Regiment, called up aged 19 in 1941, recalls his third Christmas in the forces: 'Christmas 1943 sticks in my mind as the worst. We were in a transit camp in Algiers, far from home, and whilst the food had been good so far (thanks to the skilled Army cooks), on this day there were loads and loads of us to feed and tradition had it that the officers served the men. There was no chance of turkey – just huge baths full of McConachies sloppy stew. Yuk.'

▲ 14 December 1940: an early Christmas lunch for gunners of the 289th Battery, 93rd Heavy Anti-Aircraft Regiment, Royal Artillery, based at New Ferry near Birkenhead.

PRESENTS FOR THE BOYS

The low casualty figures meant that the main concern for many families was what to send their service relatives for Christmas. In France, as in Britain, it was exceptionally cold and 'comforts for the troops' – such as knitted balaclavas, scarves and jumpers – in forces colours, either shop-bought or hand knitted, were popular with both givers and receivers.

Advertisers offered advice; the lack of action meant that the men had time on their hands, so darts and dart boards were recommended, as were board games, cards, records and books. In what might have been a hint to write home more often, fountain pens were high on the list of presents, especially good as they were small and easily sent, as well as easy to stow in a serviceman's kit.

THE GREATEST GIFT

By 1944 the armed forces had increased to 4.5 million, which included 350,000 women. They were spread over much of the world, including, after June 1940, thousands in prisoner-of-war camps in occupied Europe, North Africa and Asia. As with everything else, rationing and shortages meant that finding suitable Christmas gifts became a greater headache every year, while for servicemen and women the greatest gift of all would be Christmas leave.

SEASON'S GREETINGS

▲ *Even in 1939 people were exhorted to 'post early for Christmas'. This became a pressing need with millions of troops and evacuees away from home.*

➤ *A Civil Defence Christmas card, made from rough, unbleached, war-regulation paper, and tied with ribbon.*

The tradition of sending Christmas cards actually increased during the Second World War as many family members and friends, who ordinarily would have been seen on Christmas Day, would be away from home – either in the forces or evacuated. The absentees would also send cards back, creating large amounts of mail. The Post Office repeatedly pleaded 'post early for Christmas', especially overseas mail.

DIMINISHING SUPPLIES

At first many cards bore the badge of the sender's military unit or organization such as the Women's Land Army or Air Raid Precautions (ARP). These could be grand affairs on thick card, with gilded badges and lettering, ribbons and even photographs inside of King George VI, or another VIP inspecting the regiment. But soon, like everything else, Christmas cards suffered from shortages of materials and skilled labour.

Paper and card were particularly short as wood was needed for the war machine. In May 1940 strict paper controls were brought in for civilian use. The cards that could be bought were far smaller than before and made of cheap 'war economy' paper – thin, extremely grainy and definitely off-white. By 1943, shops, even chip shops, were no longer allowed to wrap purchases.

Christmas letters

'Send a letter to your friends this Christmas; it's much more personal. And cut out the cards to those who mean nothing at all to you. You'll save quite a bit of precious paper that way .... '

Home Chat magazine, December 1942

AIRGRAPHS AND SAVINGS CERTIFICATES

To cut down on the bulk of mail to the forces, the 'airgraph' was introduced. A message was written on a pre-printed sheet, often accompanied by a sketch; many were beautifully drawn, either

An airmail greeting home, dated 15 November 1941.

by the sender or a talented friend. It would be handed in and photographed – almost 2,000 went on a single roll of film – then enlarged and distributed at the other end. This worked both ways, so many families in Britain received airgraphs from loved ones overseas.

With the ever-increasing difficulties of finding gifts, the government came to the rescue with the savings card. The war was costing vast amounts, and to help pay for it National Savings Certificates were introduced, each costing 15 shillings (75p); a wartime shilling was the equivalent of about £1.50 today. These could be cashed in, post-war, with interest. To encourage small savers, savings stamps could be bought for as little as sixpence (2.5p) and stuck on a card. When 15 shillings-worth were accumulated they were exchanged for a savings certificate.

Silent night, holy night

Attending a church service at Christmas was another important way to reflect and remember loved ones. Brian Slemming's father was a church minister in Exeter. Brian recalls the 1943 Christmas Eve service with prisoners of war in the congregation: 'One of the POWs had asked my father ... whether he and his friends could perform a carol ... [they] walked to the front and sang *Silent Night, Holy Night*, but in German! A group of men in their humiliating uniforms who were the enemy and may, two years before, have been raining bombs on us held the congregation spellbound. Before they finished, sobs could be heard around the church, and at the end, I think that truly there was not a dry eye in the Elim Church on Paris Street. It was a moment when Christmas spirit ruled.'

The government even came up with a range of Christmas cards that were actually savings stamp cards, so the problems of both card and present could be solved by sticking inside stamps to whatever value the sender wanted to spend. Some savings cards for children were in the form of a line drawing, so that they could be coloured in.

THE GIFT THAT'S WELCOMED BY ALL

Whatever the ages, whatever the tastes of your family, friends or staff, National Savings Gift Tokens are the perfect answer to your gift problem. They're easy to buy—from any Post Office, Trustee Savings Bank, War Savings Centre or through your Savings Group, in units of 15/- up to any amount. They're easy to give—send them through the post with your Christmas greetings. They're pleasant to receive—because your gift starts to grow in value as soon as the Tokens are exchanged for Savings Certificates or used to make a deposit in the Post Office or a Trustee Savings Bank. Be in the fashion and MAKE THIS A SAVINGS CHRISTMAS.

NATIONAL SAVINGS GIFT TOKENS

By December 1943, finding presents for friends and family was a real problem. The perfect answer was a National Savings gift token, both available and patriotic.

IS YOUR JOURNEY NECESSARY?

Family get-togethers at Christmas were difficult. Petrol rationing was introduced in September 1939; car owners received enough petrol for approximately 200 miles (320km) a month, making a drive to visit relatives any distance away impractical or impossible.

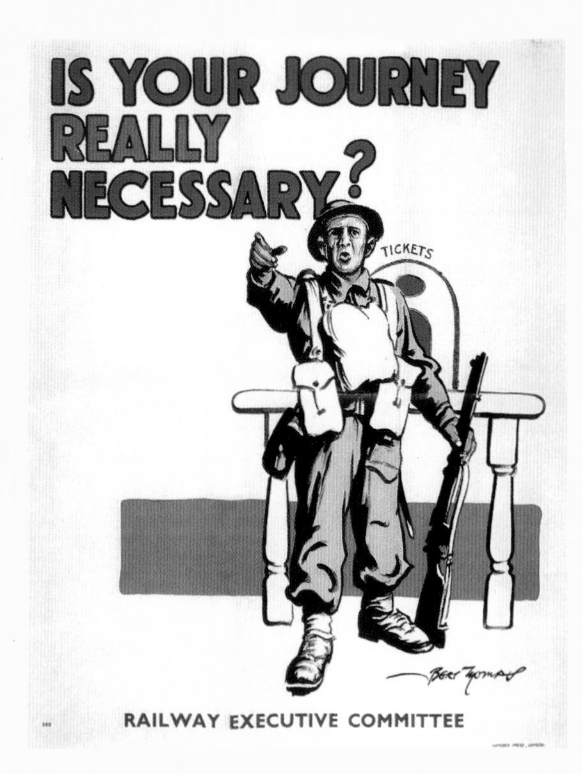

Huge overcrowding meant missed trains and great discomfort for travellers, and those not on journeys of 'national importance' were discouraged – as in this iconic poster by Bert Thomas, who was also famous for patriotic cartoons in both the First and Second World Wars.

THE BLACKOUT

Strict blackout rules were introduced on 1 September 1939, two days before war was declared. From around sunrise to sunset, all windows and doors that showed light had to be covered in a way that left no light visible from outside. Furthermore, all outside lights, including street lighting, had to be turned out.

Walking outside at night was difficult; torches were banned and even familiar routes became tricky to navigate. Motor cars could use sidelights only, with blackened reflectors, and the glass covered by two thicknesses of newspaper. Car drivers could not see pedestrians and pedestrians could not see cars. As a result the number of accidents rose steeply so within a few weeks the rules were relaxed slightly and vehicles were allowed one masked headlight. However, it was not until the introduction of a night-time speed limit of 20mph (32kph) that the accident level declined significantly.

The blackout posed a danger for rail users, where darkened stations and dimmed carriages meant getting off a train held its own perils, as this poster shows.

At least pedestrians could hear cars, which was more than could be said for bicycles, dogs, and other obstacles such as dustbins. By mid-October 1939 low-power torches with the glass covered by two layers of tissue paper could be used in the

'Cut out this Xmas fare!'

So stated a Ministry of Information advertisement in December 1943. It continued: 'This does not refer to turkey (if you can get it), or Christmas pudding (if you can make it), but to fares for travelling. The railways are heavily burdened with war traffic which must come first. To stay put is the sensible thing to do.'

street, but they had to be put out when the air-raid warning sounded.

PUBLIC TRANSPORT

Public transport fared no better at first, with lights not allowed on trains and buses. In October dimmed lights were permitted inside but, like torches, had to be extinguished when the warning sounded.

In 1940, under the threat of German invasion, signposts were removed throughout the country. By 1943 (when this cartoon was drawn), the threat was receding and signs that were not close to coastal areas were being reinstated.

Along with other items, petrol rationing became tighter and in October 1941 it was cut to a monthly average of 125 miles (200km) and in July 1942 ceased altogether. Only cars needed for the war effort received any fuel. Posters asked 'Is your journey really necessary?' or encouraged people to 'Walk short distances'. People turned to already overcrowded public transport, with trains carrying large numbers of troops and war-related freight. Things had become even more difficult after the fall of France in June 1940 when, as an anti-invasion measure, station name-boards were removed. Passengers who knew where they were were asked to inform others, but a bemused traveller enquiring where he was might find himself suspected of being a spy.

Petrol rationing forced people onto public transport, which became overcrowded, with large queues forming.

In the streets, crowds waiting for buses became so large that in April 1942 it became law that if six or more people were waiting they had to form a queue of not more than two abreast on the pavement – but this did little to soothe tempers. In the end most people gave up on all but the most necessary long-distance journeys, so that the majority of parties and family gatherings were small, local affairs.

CHRISTMAS IN THE SHELTER

Christmas 1940 came at the height of the Blitz; London had been bombed almost every night since September. In November 1940 a devastating raid on Coventry had taken place and, by Christmas, Birmingham, Manchester, Liverpool, Sheffield, Swansea, Bristol, Southampton, Portsmouth and Plymouth were among other towns and cities bombed by the Luftwaffe.

GOING UNDERGROUND

People had grown used to the warning siren and to the trudge to the air-raid shelter, either to one in their own back garden or to a public shelter.

Christmas gifts in 1940 often reflected time spent in air-raid shelters. Siren suits, books, board games and sleeping bags were all popular.

Lilliput *magazine, January 1941. The Blitz (September 1940 – May 1941) meant many people expected to spend Christmas 1940 in their Anderson shelter.*

Most expected Christmas to be no different. Women's magazines, usually full of recipes for roast turkey and Christmas pudding, this year concentrated on more practical items that might be taken to the shelter, such as sandwiches, small cakes and biscuits, while popular presents included warm clothes, sleeping bags and books.

In the event there were no raids over Christmas; the *Sunday Times* noted on Christmas Day that 'There is no report of enemy aircraft over this country last night or today; nor were there any bombing operations by the RAF last night.'

One of the great differences between having your own shelter as opposed to going to a public shelter was that you were assured of a place in your own. Another plus was that it was conveniently close, so you were far more likely to wait until the sirens went before going to the shelter. In the larger public shelters, such as the London Underground stations, places were on a 'first-come first-served' basis, so most people would go to them well before the sirens sounded to guarantee a good place. Thus, although there was no bombing over the holiday, there were still many people who spent Christmas Eve and Christmas evening in the shelter.

CREATING A CHRISTMAS COMMUNITY

In many of the larger shelters committees had been formed amongst their 'regulars', initially to keep them clean and orderly, but soon to organize entertainments. That second wartime Christmas saw many shelter parties held for local children, paid for by a whip-round amongst the regulars. In some, such as Chislehurst Caves in Kent, there were stage areas where concerts and pantomimes were performed. In others, wirelesses or gramophones were installed. Sometimes there were even pianos or, more often, people would bring along ukuleles, accordions and so on, and a sing-song took place.

London Underground staff put up Christmas trees and decorations to give a festive atmosphere. The Salvation Army toured the Underground stations giving carol concerts and handing out sweets to the children.

Many London Underground stations were used as shelters by thousands of people and at Christmas trees were put up to add festive cheer.

Christmas Eve, 1940

'We had a wooden indoor air-raid shelter at home, and during December 1940, because of the numerous air-raid warnings at night, my sister and I slept in the shelter. I can remember being in the shelter on Christmas Eve and seeing my father carrying a pillowcase full of presents in, sometime during the night. I think it was after that I started to wonder if there really was a Father Christmas!'

Jackie Burns, who was 5 years old at the time

"God rest ye merry, gentlemen, let nothing you dismay . . ."

In many shelters concerts, either planned or impromptu, took place as people sought to bring an element of normality to a very abnormal situation, as depicted in this cartoon – though at least one of the gentlemen looks less than merry!

The last major air raid of the Blitz took place on 16 May 1941, over a month before Germany attacked Russia. By Christmas 1941, with air raids being far less common, 70 per cent of all the civilian deaths throughout the war had already taken place. Few people that year, or any coming year, would celebrate Christmas in the shelter.

CHRISTMAS RATIONS

One of the greatest problems at Christmas was providing traditional food in the face of ever-increasing rationing. Before the war Britain imported around half a ton (450kg) of food per head each year; but German submarines began to sink merchant shipping almost as soon as the conflict started.

The government countered this with food rationing. In November 1939 it was announced that rationing would commence in January; no one knew or expected that it would be Britain's last ration-free Christmas for 14 years. First to be rationed were butter, bacon, ham and sugar. These were joined two months later by meat which, unlike most foods, was rationed by price, not weight. Most crucially for Christmas, the butcher had to provide customers with the set value of meat, but there was little choice in what type it was; there was no guarantee of a bird for Christmas dinner – it could easily be beef or pork.

▲ *This 'Food Facts' book from the Ministry of Food showed how to make the most of rations, and gave alternative recipes using available, non-rationed items such as potatoes and oatmeal.*

STILL MORE CUTS

In July 1940 cooking fat was added to the growing list of items 'on the ration', making the preparation of a roast chicken or joint of meat more difficult. That month the National Milk Scheme started; children below the age of five, and expectant and nursing mothers, were supplied with a pint (just under half a litre) of milk a day, while whatever was left over was shared by suppliers amongst their other customers. Later, older children would be issued with half a pint of milk a day at school, leaving even less for the general share out. This made

Novelty nourishments

'Here's a way to induce variety without having to scour every black market in the country for forbidden goodies. Try a few substitute dainties with flavours of their own next time you are racking your brains for something new. Mock dishes are no less nourishing than the ordinary, everyday foods we are so used to, but they have that small element of novelty which makes them doubly attractive to palates inclined to be bored. I'm not going to pretend that mock goose tastes exactly the same as real goose or that "chicken" cutlets would deceive a poultry keeper; but these substitutes have enough reminiscence of the real thing about them to make them very appetizing indeed and worth their weight in vitamins as a change.'

Woman magazine, December 1943

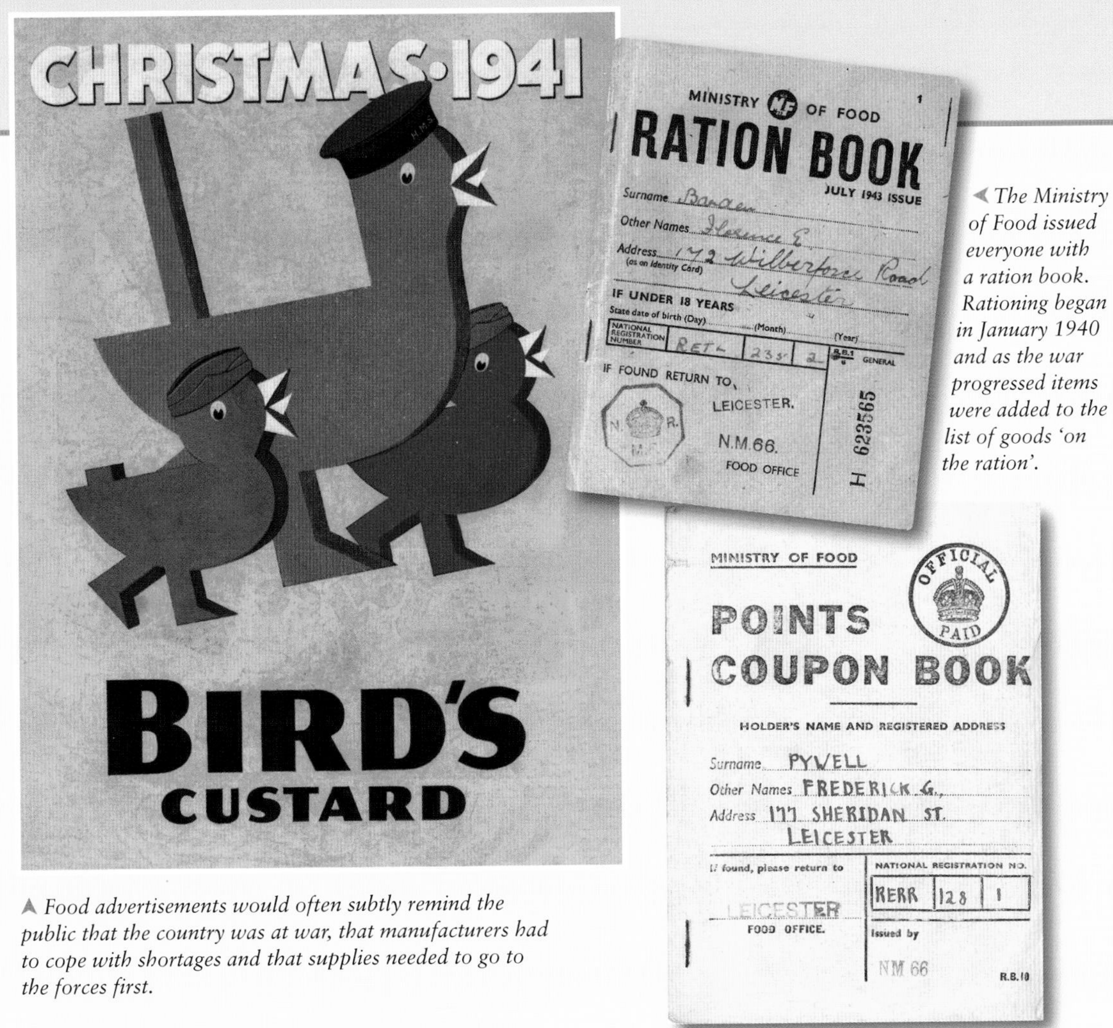

The Ministry of Food issued everyone with a ration book. Rationing began in January 1940 and as the war progressed items were added to the list of goods 'on the ration'.

Food advertisements would often subtly remind the public that the country was at war, that manufacturers had to cope with shortages and that supplies needed to go to the forces first.

In 1941 a second kind of food rationing was introduced – points rationing. As well as the basic rations everyone received a certain number of points which they could use for shortage items such as mincemeat.

recipes containing milk, such as custard and batter pudding, difficult.

In December 1940 the meat ration was reduced, although, for Christmas week only, tea was doubled to four ounces (100g) and sugar increased from eight to twelve ounces (200 to 300g). March 1941 saw preserves rationed and in October mincemeat was included in this. At the end of June an egg distribution scheme was introduced; people received one egg a week, if available. One tip when making Yorkshire puddings was to 'always add a little custard powder to the batter in these days of egg shortage'. In November 1941 National Household dried milk was brought in; this eased the problem of milk-based recipes – although housewives had to learn how to cook with it.

POINTS RATIONING

In December 1941 came the introduction of points rationing. Everyone received a book of points coupons which they could use for scarce items such as tinned salmon and, later, dried fruits and mincemeat. In March 1942 it was announced that all flour would be of the 'National wheatmeal' variety, while, in June, American powdered eggs were made available – still very limited, but some improvement on few or no eggs. As a result, wartime recipes often contained dried eggs and milk.

FESTIVE FARE

At Christmas 1943 *Parade* magazine reported: 'Norfolk and Norwich poultry wholesalers say they have been unable to buy any Christmas turkeys. There are many fine flocks of turkeys on Norfolk farms, but owners are selling to private customers and keeping the profit that would otherwise go to the wholesalers. Many local people are doubtful of their chance of getting a bird of any kind.'

TURKEY ALTERNATIVES

Recipes for Christmas dinner had to take such shortages into account. *The Woman's Magazine* in 1944 suggested: 'If you cannot have a bird of any kind, turn your joint, whatever it may be, into something resembling the succulent turkey. If your Christmas joint happens to be pork, bone and roll it, fill it with stuffing, serve apple sauce, and let bread sauce as well accompany it. Get your butcher to bone the mutton for you, if mutton is your lot, put in plenty of veal forcemeat, and serve tiny, crisply browned vegetable sausages with it. If it happens to be beef, a sage and onion stuffing is uncommonly good; serve forcemeat balls with

This photograph from December 1939 shows the central part of the Christmas dinner but, like much else, poultry would soon become something of a rarity.

The Ministry of Food tried to help housewives with advertisements, leaflets and booklets, such as this one from Christmas 1944, with recipes for Christmas fare using non-rationed goods.

Parsley and celery stuffing

4oz (100g) chopped celery, 2 large onions finely chopped, 4 level tablespoons parsley, 4oz (100g) stale breadcrumbs, salt and pepper, 2oz (50g) mixed herbs, 1oz (25g) melted dripping, hot water to mix. Mix all ingredients together adding sufficient hot water to give a soft consistency. Use for stuffing meat or poultry.

Recipe from Ministry of Food 'Festive Fare' leaflet, 1944

Mock turkey

One rabbit: to four persons.
Seasoned flour: 2 tablespoonfuls flour, ½ teaspoonful salt, ¼ teaspoonful pepper.
Savoury stuffing: 2oz (50g) breadcrumbs, 2 onions, 1 mushroom, 1 rasher fat bacon, ½oz (12g) margarine, 1 teaspoonful parsley, 1 teaspoonful sage; 1 teaspoonful mint, ½ teacupful milk, ½ teaspoonful grated lemon rind, salt, pepper and nutmeg.

Cut bacon in small pieces, remove rind; peel and chop onions and mushroom, chop herbs finely. Fry bacon, add margarine, onion, mushroom and breadcrumbs, cook together, stirring well. Add milk, boil few minutes. Season, add herbs and lemon rind. Mix well. Wash rabbit in salted water, dry and coat with seasoned flour, and stuff. Melt dripping or cooking fat, baste rabbit well, roast in moderate oven for 2 hours, basting frequently (Regulo Mark 4).

Stork margarine recipe, December 1940

Ever-tightened meat rations led people to look for alternatives. One popular way was to keep rabbits in the back garden, and there were books to help.

the stuffed beef. The humble rabbit, stuffed and roasted, with plenty of brown gravy and sausages or sausage-meat balls, really makes a fine dish, and for its filling you can use either sage and onion or veal forcemeat. Remember the bread sauce!'

MEAT-FREE SUGGESTIONS

Not everyone was upset by the shortages of meat; vegetarianism had become popular in the 1930s, as part of a healthy living movement. Vegetarians could register as such, and receive extra cheese and nuts instead of the meat ration. As early as November 1939 the London Vegetarian Society issued recipes for 'A wartime vegetarian Christmas dinner', starting with onion and turnip soup with wholemeal dinner rolls, followed by steamed chestnut roll with tomato sauce, Brussels sprouts, braised carrots and baked potatoes, and finishing off with Christmas pudding with honey and lemon sauce and mince pies. As the war progressed, however, it was not only vegetarians who would go meatless.

'There won't be many turkeys this year', or indeed many to come; a Ministry of Food advertisement from Christmas 1941 suggested how to make the most of Christmas dinner without one.

MORE FESTIVE FARE

Fat, in the form of butter or margarine, for cakes and puddings was in very short supply; butter was among the first rationed items in January 1940 at 4oz (100g) per person per week. It remained around this level for most of the war and indeed long after. Margarine was also rationed. The combined ration for butter and margarine usually totalled 6oz (150g), with at least 2oz (50g) of that being margarine.

Home-made sweets and Christmas cakes, December 1939. Such lavish icing, requiring lots of soon-to-be-rationed sugar, would not be seen again for many years.

PARAFFIN AND COCOA

One common alternative to fat for baking was to use paraffin. Apparently it tasted all right, but you did need to stay near a toilet for some hours after eating it!

Bird's Custard advertisement, December 1939: food rationing would begin within a few weeks and soon the ingredients for such a traditional Christmas pudding would be hard, if not impossible, to get hold of.

To give a Christmas pudding its rich dark colour, a Ministry of Food recipe from December 1943 suggested adding cocoa powder, and combining syrup with gravy browning if the more traditional black treacle was unavailable.

A country Christmas

People living on farms were more fortunate in what foodstuffs were available during the war. Brian Martin lived on a farm in Suffolk: 'We had eggs, milk and poultry. We bought a turkey for Christmas and pickled a pig just before it. Every Christmas one of our neighbours would come to dinner and tea ... After [the King's speech] our neighbour would go home to feed his animals and we would feed ours, collect the eggs, and shut the poultry huts up when it was dark to keep the foxes out ... Soon after Christmas we would have tea and spend the evening with some of our neighbours in turn ... in one house I remember a bowl of large lumps of bomb-damaged chocolate that was sent for animal food.'

Blackberry mincemeat

Housewives who planned ahead could make use of autumn fruits to make blackberry mincemeat for Christmas mince pies with this recipe from *Woman* magazine:

'Allow to every pound of blackberries (bottled), 4 large cooking apples, 4oz [100g] suet or shredded margarine, 4oz [100g] nuts, 8 drops almond essence, ½lb [400g] dried fruit (figs, dates, sultanas, currants, raisins, or a mixture of these), 2 level teaspoonfuls mixed spice, a little honey. Bake or steam apples for preference, then mash pulp, add berries, spice and almond essence, put in pan over slow heat and cook slowly for ¼ hour. Cool off before adding shredded suet or margarine. Chop or mince fruit and add, also chopped nuts, and mix well. Cover with warmed honey, then pot and seal. This keeps very well.'

The answer to this mother's dilemma was a Mrs Peek's Christmas pudding; from a Peek Frean's advertisement, December 1940.

MARZIPAN AND ICING

Even if the ingredients were found for a Christmas cake, there was still the problem of how to marzipan and ice it. With ground almonds difficult to come by, mock marzipan could be made using: ½lb (200g) haricot beans, 4 tablespoons sugar, 2 tablespoons ground rice, 1 tablespoon almond essence, 1 tablespoon margarine. The method involved soaking the beans for 24 hours, then cooking until tender before putting them in a tin in a warm oven until dry and floury. After being rubbed through a sieve the sugar was beaten into the bean puree, the ground rice, warmed margarine and flavouring added, and all beaten until smooth.

The Ministry of Food solved the problem of icing with a recipe using sugar, dried milk and water. Their recipe included this footnote: 'This icing does not keep very well, and so should be put on just before desired.' When they said it did not keep, they meant it – it had a nasty tendency to slowly disappear into the cake.

This December 1942 advertisement from Stork margarine summed up the problems of Christmas cooking.

SWEET TREATS

Sugar was among the first items to be rationed in January 1940; consequently sweets became increasingly scarce until July 1942 when they went 'on the ration' at the rate of two ounces (50g) a week. By October this had risen to 12 ounces (300g) a month, where it remained until sweet rationing stopped in April 1949 – only to recommence four months later, and not ending until 1953. In wartime, even the sweets you could get were 'zoned' – available only in areas near where they were manufactured.

SWEET MEMORIES

Such a small ration of sweets had to be eked out – the makers of Mars bars (one bar was a week's ration) suggested you cut it in slices. Most children, however, did not waste their ration on a single bar of chocolate; they preferred to buy small sweets such as hundreds and thousands, dolly mixtures or sherbet, which could be made to last by taking a small pinch at a time. June Fiddler recalls: 'We used to buy the smallest sweets we could, pear drops and so on, so that you got a lot of them.' Pear drops were Margaret Pilgrim's favourites: 'I got nine of them a week with my ration, which was one a day Monday to Friday and two on Saturday and two on Sunday!' Barratts responded to the situation by bringing out the 'Ration bag'. This contained three ounces (75g) of mixed sweets and a novelty, such as a cardboard mask; the idea worked so well that the bags continued long after rationing ended, renamed the 'Jamboree bag'.

In December 1939, Mackintosh advertised Quality Street as 'A joyful assortment of toffees and chocolates packed in fancy boxes'; by 1944 they were advertising their big tins of sweets as 'something to look forward to' after the war.

With the shortage of fresh frui the Ministry of Food encouraged people to eat carrots as a rich source of vitamin C. This humbl vegetable could be used in carro cakes, Christmas puddings – an even treacle toffee carrots.

Marzipan potatoes

2oz (50g) margarine, 1/4lb (100g) each granulated sugar and soya flour, 2 small teaspoonfuls almond essence, 2 tablespoonfuls water, cocoa.
Put the margarine in a saucepan and set over low heat. When melted add the sugar, water and almond essence and stir all together for about a minute, being careful not to let it brown or burn. Take the pan off the heat, stir in the soya flour, mix well, then turn on to a pastry board dusted with cocoa and sifted sugar, and knead well for at least 2 minutes. The paste is then ready to be shaped into potatoes, and they should be rolled in cocoa when made and pricked with a fork to give 'eyes'.

Recipe from *The Woman's Magazine*, 1944

◀ Wartime sweets included many that are still popular today, such as Bassetts Liquorice Allsorts and Rowntree's Fruit Gums.

▶ This December 1941 advertisement reminded readers that 'Chocolate is scarce'; soon large boxes of chocolates such as this would be a thing of the past.

HOME-MADE CHOCOLATE

The traditional present of a box of chocolates was a thing of the past, but you could make your own, and the magazines came up with a variety of recipes. Milk chocolate, for example, could be made from: 2 dessertspoonfuls golden syrup, 2 heaped teaspoonfuls cocoa, 2 dessertspoonfuls dried milk. The method read: 'Warm the syrup until it runs like water. Mix the cocoa and the dried milk well together, then pour on the syrup. Beat together thoroughly. Spread mixture on a greased tin. When quite cold, remove from tin and cut into squares.'

The spirit of Christmas

'Perhaps just because this is another war Christmas, you want to make things as old-time Christmassy as possible. There won't be any luxuries of course. We all know that men and ships are needed on far more important work than to bring us unessential foods. But the spirit of Christmas transforms simple, homely things. To see the children's delight is more than worth the little trouble of shaping biscuit pastry into little men, or toys and animals, and dotting them with sultanas or currants for eyes, nose and mouth; or of crushing a few boiled sweets and sprinkling them over the trifle or custard.'

Ministry of Food, December 1943

DECK THE HALLS

Some Christmas decorations were carefully packed and brought out every year, and others were purchased annually: balloons, paper chains and, of course, the tree. A few families had artificial trees (many made in Germany) but most would buy a real tree.

Wood became a shortage item almost immediately; vast amounts were needed for the war effort. Even by Christmas 1939 trees were in short supply and became more scare as the war progressed. Likewise paper for decorations – by mid-1940 there were tight controls on its use, while, with the fall of the Malayan plantations to the Japanese in 1942, rubber was very tightly limited for civilian use, so there were no balloons.

DECORATIVE IDEAS

Decorations became do-it-yourself. Paper chains could be made by cutting strips of coloured paper from old magazines, which kept children occupied for a few hours in the run-up to Christmas. In country areas, holly and ivy were usually easy to come by, and to some extent mistletoe. However, in towns and cities suitable trees and bushes were often virtually stripped bare. In 1941 *Woman & Home* suggested a yuletide log as a table decoration: 'Choose a small, chubby log from the garden or wood-cupboard and distemper it white, here and there, to give the semblance of snow. A sprinkle of Epsom Salts or similar salts will give the effect of frost, and then all that is needed is a sprig of holly and a bright red silk "tie-up".'

The cover of Housewife *magazine in December 1944 showed this imaginary scene of a window with Christmas decorations. In reality, even though the blackout rules were being eased, a lighted window such as this would have brought the air-raid wardens running.*

Traditional 1940s Christmas decorations included concertina-style balls, bells and garlands.

▲ *Putting up decorations, 1939. Balloons and Chinese lanterns are being added to by the latest decorative idea – coloured cellophane. The woman on the stepladder is dressed in an up-to-the-minute siren suit.*

DIY Christmas tree

'Christmastide will soon be with us, and though it is uncertain whether this feast will be one of real rejoicing or not, I feel sure readers will want some simple form of Christmas decoration. Here is a modern Christmas tree, which the handyman can make. There is a wooden base, and a square pole to which the triangles of various sizes, made of plywood, are fixed. If plywood is not obtainable, owing to war conditions, good strong cardboard will do equally well. The finished production is painted bright green, and decorated with stars and moons cut out from tinfoil of various colours and patterns and stuck on. The effect can be enhanced by strings of silver beads hung from the triangles, while on Christmas Day, when the tree is loaded with presents, electrically illuminated magic lanterns and fairy lights make it a most attractive novelty.'

Practical Mechanics, December 1940

◄ Practical Mechanics *magazine, December 1940, showed how to make this very modernist design tree using either plywood or cardboard.*

In 1943 *Woman's Own* had this idea for its readers: 'To frost evergreen branches for decoration, take a jam jar one-third full of gum arabic and add a little boiling water, leave for some hours until dissolved and then add the same quantity of Epsom Salts. Stand the jar in hot water and stir until the salts have dissolved, then apply quickly with a paint brush.'

Even the smallest, most threadbare tree cost a fortune on the black market, as did artificial trees. *Woman's Own* in 1943 suggested: 'Shortage of Christmas tree decorations can be overcome by tying bows of different coloured ribbon on the branches, looks fun and any short length of ribbon can be used.' Alternatively, blown light bulbs could be painted and hung from the branches. Other tree decorations could be made from paper, pipe cleaners, scraps of wood and especially coloured cellophane, such as sweet wrappers. Pictures from old Christmas cards or magazines were also cut out and hung from Christmas trees.

POPULAR PRESENTS

In December 1939 shops were still full of goods which would later become scarce or disappear altogether; that first wartime Christmas the problem when choosing a present was picking the right gift. Magazines offered their usual advice, while manufacturers' advertisements displayed the gifts on offer. There were traditional favourites: cigarettes and cigars, chocolates, cosmetics, perfume, clothes and jewellery, the latter brought up-to-date with the introduction of 'sweetheart' items – such as brooches and pendants – in the form of miniature regimental or service badges. These could be bought in base metal and coloured glass, or even gold and platinum set with precious stones.

IDEAL ID GIFTS

Another war-related item was the identity bracelet. People were urged to carry identification, so that should they be injured or killed in an air raid their next of kin could be contacted. Many outlets sold identification bracelets – as chain bracelets for women and on leather straps for men, or in the form of a pendant.

▲ *Presents for all the family, December 1939, including a 'Service Pack' recommended for a brother.*

▲ *This December 1939 advertisement features a very rare sight – Father Christmas smoking a cigarette. The majority of adults smoked at this time, when the health dangers were unrecognized.*

Waste not, want not

'We feel quite sure that much more paper would be saved if every room had its own waste paper bin, even the kitchen. So we're suggesting that you should give some of your friends waste paper baskets this Christmas, and so indirectly help on the waste paper salvage campaign.'

Home Chat magazine, Christmas 1942

Similarly, there were wallets which incorporated a panel for an identity card. In September 1939 everyone was issued with an ID card, production of which could be demanded by the police or, from May 1940, Local Defence Volunteers (the LDV, later known as the Home Guard). Wallets manufactured later in the war might have pockets for ration books.

GAS-MASK CASES AND SIREN SUITS

Other wartime-themed gifts included gas-mask cases. Gas masks had been issued in cardboard boxes, which, with a length of string, made a carrying case. These were neither robust, weatherproof, nor particularly attractive, and many firms sold alternative cases, from cheap Rexine versions through to handbags which had a compartment for a gas mask.

There were also helmets – often Bakelite or fibre versions of the army helmet – and a version of the overall known as the siren suit or shelter suit, designed to keep the wearer warm in the air-raid shelter during raids. These items became even more desirable for Christmas 1940, when the German bombing offensive was at its height. Prime Minister Winston Churchill, who was a famous siren-suit wearer, even presented one to King George VI for Christmas that year!

INCREASING SHORTAGES

However, it was the traditional gifts which were most popular, and remained so as rationing and shortages began to bite ever deeper. Once-common articles such as a box of chocolates, a packet of cigarettes, a bottle of whisky, a pair of stockings, or a box of face powder became difficult or even impossible to find.

By December 1944 there was little left in the shops that did not require coupons. But, as Webbs' Seeds pointed out, many people were 'digging for victory' so vegetable seeds were a popular gift solution.

As the war dragged on, the U-boat menace continued to choke Britain's much-needed imports and the war effort demanded ever-more raw materials; supplies of luxuries to the Home Front dried up, then even basic necessities became short, and Christmas presents reflected this.

Beauty box

'It's a pretty beauty box and it's packed full of good ideas. The box itself is just an old shoe-box covered with gay packing paper. Inside we've filled it with all the beauty items that every girl needs, and often finds hard to get nowadays. Good side combs are hard to find, but if you manage to get a couple for your girl friend, trim them with bright ribbon bows.'

Woman magazine, December 1943

HOME-MADE GIFTS

Although Christmas 1939 was pretty much 'business as usual' as far as giving presents was concerned, as the war progressed a number of factors contrived to make gift-buying very difficult.

The first of these was rationing; food, clothes, soap and sweets were 'on the ration', making many traditional presents a thing of the past. People barely had enough coupons for their own needs, let alone spares for presents. Second were shortages; imported food and goods, especially raw materials, became scarce. Civilian 'luxuries' came bottom of the list of priorities. At the same time, factories were turning from production of goods for the home market to war materials.

Raffia was used to make this table crumb set, including the brush itself.

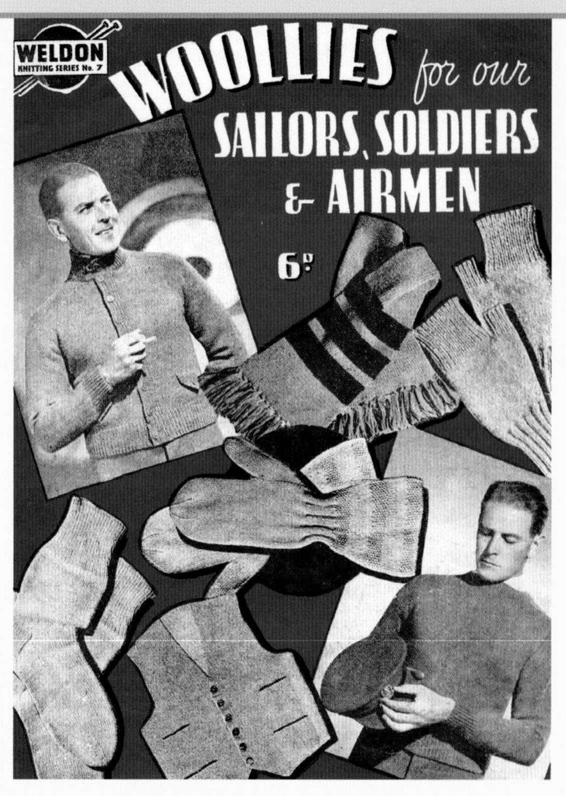

A wartime knitting pattern for 'Woollies for our sailors, soliders and airmen'.

All this had the effect of pushing up prices. The government tried to counter this with price controls, but this simply diverted many items to the black market, where shortage goods could be got – for a price!

The problem of high prices for luxuries was added to by the government. The enormous cost of the war was paid for with ever-increasing taxes.

The humblest of gifts

'Let us make the most of the Christmas that is almost upon us. My presents are ready – just odds and ends contrived from scraps of wool such as egg-cosies, tea-cosies, gloves, ration-card cases, to say nothing of string shopping bags. That's one good thing the war has done, you know, it's made us all quite thrilled to receive the humblest of gifts, and we really do value things because of the thought behind them, and the effort entailed, rather than for their splendour.'

Home Chat magazine, December 1943

Despite being rationed, tea continued to be a staple comfort throughout the war. A hand-knitted tea cosy to keep the teapot warm could be made from very little wool and was a welcome gift.

Taxes took up 25 per cent of private income in 1939, rising to 36 per cent in 1944. In October 1940 purchase tax was introduced on many goods, at rates varying from 16 to 33 per cent. In 1942 purchase tax on a number of items doubled to 66⅔ per cent, and in 1943 rose to 100 per cent!

MAKE DO AND MEND

With the introduction of clothes rationing in 1941, people were encouraged to 'make do and mend': repairing old items or using them to make new clothes. Knitting became a favourite pastime, as old items could be unravelled and the wool reused to make new clothes, so scarves and jumpers became popular gifts.

Magazines were full of ideas for home-made gifts. Empty treacle or dried milk tins were useful; with a hole cut in the lid they made a handy cottonwool dispenser, or with several small holes became a powder or flour dispenser, the whole painted or covered with pretty paper.

Pretty and practical

'There's still some Christmas wrapping paper in the shops. But don't waste it on tying up presents. Instead, buy a cheap hearth-brush, cover the woodwork with the gay paper, pasting it on carefully, and there's a nice little gift for a house-proud friend.'

Home Chat magazine, December 1942

Jewellery was especially difficult to obtain, yet with clothes rationed a colourful necklace or brooch could transform an often-worn dress. Old silver cutlery could be shaped into bracelets, while felt could be fashioned into brooches, necklaces, belts and earrings. Beads could be made from papier-mâché, brightly painted, or fancy buttons strung on a leather bootlace to form a necklace. Wood or scrap pieces of plastic could be shaped into brooches, using safety pins or men's collar pins as clasps.

Yet as the war dragged on most sources of such reusable materials began to dry up, and by 1944 the magazines found even their inventiveness pushed to its limits.

A brooch of beads in different sizes and a novel necklet quickly made of pretty buttons

Jewellery was a favoured DIY present. All sorts of scraps were utilized: old silver cutlery, strands of wool, wood, plastic or, as for this necklet and brooch, buttons and beads.

FOR THE CHILDREN

At Christmas 1939 the shortages of goods which would become such a feature of life were hardly manifesting themselves. Shops had the full range of tin soldiers, tanks and cannons, though now brought up to date with anti-aircraft guns, searchlights and even barrage balloons. To these were added dolls in service uniform, and child-size outfits for the various services, including a Red Cross nurse's uniform for girls. To complete the look there were children's tin helmets. It is interesting to note that many of the toys on sale that year bore the legend 'made in Germany'.

WHAT WOULD SANTA BRING?

Of course the usual favorites – dolls, teddy bears and pedal cars – remained popular, especially for the younger children who tended to be protected from any mention of the war. By Christmas 1940, however, children in Britain's towns and cities could no longer be insulated from the war, with the German air assault at its height. Reg Parks, aged 8 in 1940, was concerned about Father Christmas: 'What with the ack-ack [anti-aircraft] guns, searchlights and all, I was worried he wouldn't come, but Mum said he would, though he wouldn't be able to carry so many toys on his sleigh.'

Life in the air-raid shelter had become the norm and gifts that year reflected this. Popular presents included those which could help while away long hours in the shelters. Card games and board games were high on the list, as well as books, jigsaws and other puzzles. Warm clothing would also feature, most fashionably in the form of a child's siren suit.

▲ *Frog model aircraft and Tri-ang toys were still available in 1941, albeit in short supply. Many of the toys shown here are war-related – even the clockwork tractor is an RAF model.*

◄ *This pattern for ragdolls in various service outfits dates from early in the war. The female doll is a nurse, though later she might have been dressed in an ATS, WAAFs or Wrens uniform.*

Mend a friend

'Now that toys are so scarce and expensive it is well worthwhile looking out those which are still fairly good and will stand a little renovation. Toys of the furry type can be given a dry-cleaning bath. Put some bran in a tin in the oven, or the fire, and when it is hot rub it well into the coat of the animal with the finger-tips. Afterwards rub with a clean cloth dipped in the bran. When the fur is clean, shake and beat well until all the bran is removed and finish off by combing the surface with a very fine comb. Animals that have lost their eyes can be fitted with small button-moulds, painted in bright colours. New ears can be made with oddments of coloured felt, and if you cannot match the colour, replace both ears.'

Home Chat magazine, December 1942

HARD-TO-COME-BY TOYS

Grumbling about the inflated prices being charged for toys reached a crescendo as they became shortage items. The supply of German-made and other imported toys dried up, while most British toy manufacturers were now producing war materials instead. Those that remained suffered from shortages of raw materials as the Home Front went to the bottom of the pile for supplies.

MECCANO

AND

HORNBY TRAINS

The World's Greatest Toys

We regret that we cannot supply these famous toys today, but they will be ready for you again after the war. In the meantime, if you are in any difficulties with your toys, write to

MECCANO LIMITED, BINNS ROAD, LIVERPOOL 13

◄ *By December 1943, like many other pre-war toys, Meccano and Hornby trains were no longer available, but many manufacturers continued to advertise their goods as something to look forward to after the war.*

The black market flourished – scarce toys could be obtained, at an inflated price, if you knew who to see. Those without either the desire or the cash to use this avenue were forced to explore other alternatives. Christmas gift shopping became an all-year round occupation – when a supply of any hard-to-come-by items such as toys became available in a shop, a queue soon formed outside.

Old toys were often recycled – a fresh coat of paint or a good clean could work wonders. Good prices could be charged for second-hand toys and books; by the end of the war such items could fetch more than they had cost new, and even jigsaw puzzles with missing pieces were saleable. Another widespread answer was to make presents.

▼ *National Fire Service personnel making toys. This was done in their spare time, often from materials salvaged from fires, and the toys given to children at Christmas parties in hospitals or nurseries.*

PARTIES FOR GROWN-UPS

In 1939 the blackout made travel difficult at night, so parties were often held earlier in the day. However, going out in the dark became safer as the war progressed; because the amount of petrol allowed by rationing was first cut in 1941, then stopped altogether in 1942, there were far fewer vehicles on the roads. But venturing out after dark remained something to be avoided if possible.

RAISING A GLASS

In the first few months of the war alcohol was still easy to come by, and a Cointreau advertisement recommended these cocktails: the 'Silent Third' (⅓ Cointreau, ⅓ Scotch whisky, ⅓ lemon juice); and the 'Mainbrace' (⅓ Cointreau, ⅓ gin, ⅓ grapefruit juice).

By Christmas 1940, however, problems were compounded by food rationing, making catering difficult – how to make sandwiches for 20 people with two ounces of butter and four ounces of margarine? In the towns and cities the problem was further complicated by bombing and the fact that most evenings were spent in air-raid shelters. Some people shared shelters with friends and neighbours, taking it in turn to visit each other, and many had wind-up gramophones or battery-powered radios.

Alcohol was becoming harder to find, especially spirits, and recipes for drinks reflected this, such as the 'Shandy Gaff' (equal measures of ginger beer and pale ale, served ice cold). Christmases after 1940 saw little air-raiding, but shortages, including the supply of alcohol, were really biting. The *Daily Mirror* in 1941 reported: 'The Christmas drink

➤ *Moussec advertisement, December 1939. Shortages of alcohol were soon to be another blow for parties.*

Make 'PLUM DELIGHTS' for your party!

1 bottle plums,
1¾ oz. Brown & Polson Cornflour,
3 tablespoons water,
stale cake crumbs.

Stew fruit with sugar as required; when soft, rub all through sieve. Measure quantity and make it up to 1-pint with water. Put into pan to heat.

Mix cornflour with the water; add to puree, stir till boiling, boil 3 minutes, stirring well. Remove from the heat, beat vigorously for a few minutes.

A little orange or lemon cordial will improve the flavour.

Put some stale cake crumbs into bottom of sundae glasses, pour mixture over, leave to set. Then, decorate as liked.

A few blanched plum kernels, or sifted cake crumbs, make an effective decoration.

■ For hints on Xmas Cooking, send 1d. stamp to: Mrs. Jean Scott, Cookery Service Dept., 20, Stratford Place, London, W.1.

BROWN & POLSON CORNFLOUR

Has helped housewives for a hundred years.

Issued by Brown & Polson, Ltd.

◀ *This party-food recipe from December 1943 features stale cake crumbs amongst its modest ingredients.*

Party dresses for women and girls, December 1939. The lack of air raids that first wartime Christmas, and as yet no rationing, meant that there were plenty of parties.

One way of having a new dress for Christmas in times of clothes rationing was to knit your own, as with this example from 1944.

shortage gave profiteers a chance to charge what they liked. But lots of people couldn't get beer at any price.' Most parties were small, bring a bottle (and some food) affairs.

OUTFITS AND GAMES

Clothes rationing meant a new party dress would have been out of the question by Christmas 1941; women could probably only afford one new dress a year. However, the 'make do and mend' initiative came to the rescue; women's magazines were full of ideas for smartening up an old frock or blouse, while rare treasures such as a pair of stockings or some make-up, carefully put away for a special occasion, might be brought out for the festivities, especially if a loved one was coming home on leave. It also became the norm for friends to borrow clothes from each other for parties or dances.

But there were other ways to enjoy a party; it was still traditional to play games at Christmas, even at adult parties. In 1939 *Good Housekeeping* magazine told its readers: 'Every party is a success if you play amusing games.'

'Bedtime' game

'On a table at one end of the room put two boxes of matches, two candles in candlesticks and two old cushions to represent babies. The players divide into two equal teams at one end of the room. At the word "Go" the first players run to the table, light a candle, grab the baby and carry both back to their team, passing all the way round it and then proceeding back to the table. Here they put down the baby, blow out the candle and run back to their places. The next player then follows on and does exactly the same. The first team back in its original place is the winner. Needless to say, any player whose candle blows out before it should must return to the table, light it up and begin the putting to bed all over again.'

Good Housekeeping magazine, 1939

PARTIES FOR CHILDREN

People worked extremely hard to make Christmas special for the children. In 1939 well over one million young evacuees were away from home. Many local authorities, including the London County Council, paid for parties for their evacuees, while sympathy for the children far from home meant that other parties were paid for by local organizations. Such functions were also arranged for local youngsters by bodies such as the ARP (Air Raid Precautions) or the fire service. With the onset of the bombing, these get-togethers in target areas were regarded as dangerous, but once the raids settled down to a routine of night-bombing, parties were held in the afternoon.

The arrival of the 'Yanks' in 1942 was an eye-opener; the American servicemen came bearing long-disappeared luxuries, such as sweets, ice cream and chewing gum – and would be met with the cry, 'Got any gum chum?' Many US bases organized Christmas parties for local children, where they would be showered with such treats.

CHILDREN'S GAMES

Besides food and sweets, successful parties had to include games, including the old favourites such as pass the parcel, musical chairs, blind man's buff and nuts in May. *The Girl's Own Paper* of December 1944 gave these directions for a game: 'Divide your players into as many equal groups as possible, each group representing one animal – if you have five in a group, then you will have five dogs, five cats and so on. Each group

▲ *A Christmas 1939 party held for London County Council evacuees. Many local children were envious that the 'vacees' received such treats.*

◀ *The* Girl's Own Paper *of December 1944 shows young women getting ready for a Christmas party. Rationing, air raids and the blackout had made parties far rarer, and definitely something to look forward to.*

Just William

'We want to be 'vacuated too,' said Arabella Simpkin, a red-haired long-nosed girl, who automatically constituted herself the leader of any group of which she formed part. 'They get all the fun ...'
'Yes,' grumbled Frankie Miller, a small stout, snub-nosed boy of seven. 'They got a Christmas party an' a Christmas tree.'
'An' tins of sweets all round,' put in Ella Poppleham, a morose-looking child, with a shock of black hair and a squint. 'A whole tin of sweets each. It's not fair it isn't. Puttin' on side an' havin' parties an' eatin' whole tins of sweets. It's not fair. We oughter be 'vacuated, too.'

From *William and the Evacuees* by Richmal Crompton, 1940

has a leader, who is provided with a paper bag. Turn all your animals out of the room, and hide lots of nuts – any small object will do if you can't get nuts, but they must all be the same. The animals come in, and search for the hidden objects. When a dog finds whatever is hidden, he remains beside without touching it, and barks at the top of his voice, and so on. The leader of the dog group comes and puts it in her paper bag. The group whose leader has the most of the hidden objects in the bag has won.'

With Father Christmas on war service, Mother Christmas is taking his place at this party for nursery children.

Santa in a jeep

In December 1944 US serviceman Wally Hoffman was a member of a B17 'Flying Fortress' bomber crew stationed at Polebrook, near Peterborough. A gala Christmas party planned for local children was delayed until the New Year due to the 'Battle of the Bulge'. Wally recalls: 'Santa Clause arrived (by Jeep) and ... gave each [child] a bag containing candy, candy bars, oranges, apples, and bananas. [For the] delayed Christmas dinner ... there was the usual turkey, stuffing, mashed potatoes, sweet potatoes, cranberries, and pumpkin pie. When we took our charges full of turkey to the busses to take them home I can still see that permanent smile on their little faces as they clutched their toys and waved goodbye ... It made up for not being home for Christmas.'

MORE FESTIVE FUN

At the outbreak of war, entertainment was the last thing on the government's mind. The fledgling BBC television service was shut down on 1 September 1939, and two days later the scheduled wireless programmes were replaced by news bulletins and official announcements interspersed with organ music.

Cinemas and theatres were closed in case of heavy bombing but, with the failure of the Luftwaffe to appear, there was a public outcry and the government was forced to allow them to reopen, with earlier closing times. The BBC responded by bringing back its entertainment programmes, including such pre-war favourites as *Band Waggon*, starring Arthur Askey and Richard 'Stinker' Murdoch, and *It's That Man Again* (now re-christened *ITMA*, in a reference to the military-style acronyms which had arrived with the war), starring Tommy Handley.

King George VI making a radio broadcast in 1939.

By Christmas the wireless was back in its stride, with variety shows, talks, and concerts of classical and popular music, with one new addition. It was not a regular custom at that time to have a 'King's Speech' on Christmas Day, but that first Christmas of the war the government was keen for the sovereign to broadcast to the nation and the Empire, for purposes of morale. Although he had given his first Christmas broadcast as king two years previously, George VI, who had a speech impediment, was definitely not keen, but in the end gave in; his speech was well received.

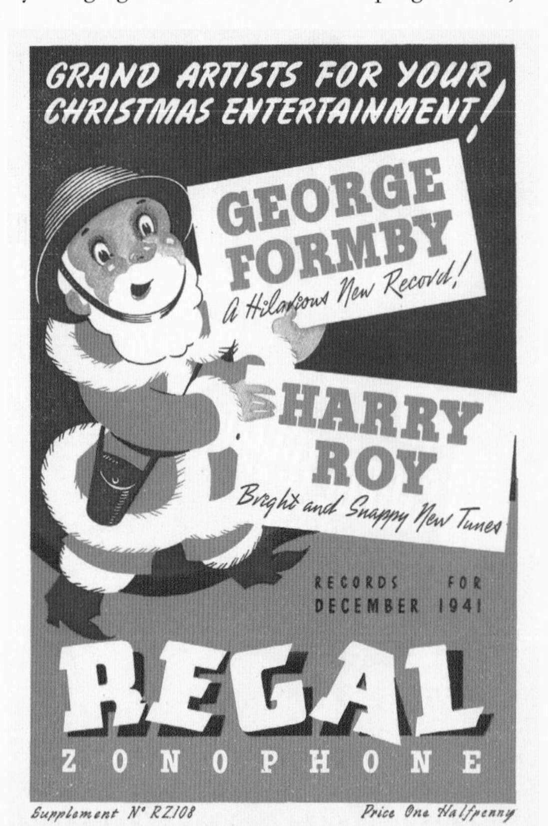

Regal records advertisement, Christmas 1941. Harry Roy, with his Tiger Ragamuffins, was one of the top bandleaders, while George Formby was the leading cinema box-office star with films like Let George Do It.

Keep calm, the show will go on

'Patrons will be informed if an air raid warning has been given. If an air raid warning is given, keep calm, the show will go on. You are safer here than in the street. If you wish to leave, please go quietly. Please keep your gas mask on your lap, and do not put it under the seat.'

Notice in a theatre programme, 1939

FRANCIS LAIDLER'S
Magnificent Comedy Pantomime

MOTHER GOOSE

TWO PERFORMANCES DAILY
1.30 AND 5.30

Carol singing

'I must have been a very precocious child as I remember on a couple of occasions insisting that the Christmas spirit should be invoked with a carol singing session. A neighbouring lone mother and her three children were invited in to sing with us. The embarrassment on the faces of all the adults present and the excruciating sound we made have long stuck in my memory.'

Joyce Gibson, a child during the war

◀ *The cover of the programme for* Mother Goose *at the Coliseum in Charing Cross, London, dating from 1942/3. The pantomime starred Patricia Burke as 'Colin, a village boy' and Billy Dainty as 'Asbestos, the donkey'.*

▼ *Illusionist Kardoma's act originally involved filling the stage with flowers but the 'Dig for Victory' campaign meant vegetables were grown on any available space. Kardoma changed his flowers to flags and advertised his act as 'Keeping the flags flying'. Such patriotic entertainment was very popular during the war.*

'HE'S BEHIND YOU!'

That popular form of Christmas entertainment in Britain – the pantomime – was in question in 1939. But there was a determination, especially with the 'Phoney War' at its peak, that the hostilities would not stop Christmas, resulting in a bumper crop of pantos starring the big names of British entertainment, such as Arthur Askey, George Formby and Sandy Powell.

By Christmas 1940 the Blitz was at its height, but the initial shock had mostly worn off and many people resolved not be cowed. Once again pantomimes, along with local variety shows, were staged in village halls and large public shelters. Scripts, as ever, had topical references such as rationing and the blackout. The most popular characters were the villains, usually sporting a Hitler moustache and his familiar fringe.

For most, however, Christmas entertainment was enjoyed at home and featured the wireless, the gramophone or a sing-song. It was still usual to have a piano in the front room, and there was generally someone who could knock out the popular tunes: *Run Rabbit Run*, *We'll Meet Again* and *When Can I have a Banana Again?*

PEACETIME CHRISTMAS 1945

May 1945, and the surrender of Germany meant the end of fighting in Europe. The surrender of Japan in August brought the war to a complete end, but many of its day-to-day effects carried on. Everyone had looked forward to peace for so long that, when it came, it was inevitably something of an anticlimax.

The return of the troops took a long time; many had to wait until 1946. Physical and mental scars took time to heal, and families had to be rebuilt, with many younger children not knowing their returning fathers. And of course there were many families where there were now permanent gaps around the table.

Even in the late 1940s, post-war Christmases were still 'make do and mend' affairs. Shortages and rationing continued, and indeed got worse, with bread rationed and potatoes in short supply, while the extremely cold winter of 1947 tested the country's depleted coal stocks and worn-out public transport to their limits. It was not until 1953 that Britain was able to celebrate a mostly ration-free Christmas once more, though meat rationing did not end for another six months.

The Victory Twins, appropriately named Vic and Vicky, 'gaily stepping out at the head of the Christmas toy procession' in outfits that could be adapted for fancy dress. From the Girl's Own Paper, *December 1945.*

Yet the question remains: was Christmas diminished by the privations of war? For many the answer would be no, for stripped of the commercial aspects the spirit of Christmas remained, and was, if anything, strengthened. With ever-increasing shortages presents were lovingly hand-made, or the result of hours of window-shopping and long queues: the thought really did count. 'Peace on earth' became not merely a phrase, but the deepest desire of those subjected to repeated bombing, or worried about evacuated children, or husbands, sons or daughters in the forces. An old-fashioned family Christmas became another dream.

In a time of immense upheaval, Christmas remained a constant; a link with the past and a promise of better times to come.